A WEEKEND WITH ROUSSEAU

A WEEKEND WITH
ROUSSEAU

By Gilles Plazy

RIZZOLI
NEW YORK

A tiny little bird
On the shoulder of an angel
Together they sing the praise
Of sweet Rousseau

Sweet Rousseau
You are the angel
And you are the bird
That sing your praises

—Guillaume Apollinaire

Entrez! Come in! I love weekends, don't you? I'm delighted that we can spend this one together. No music or art lessons to teach! My friends used to call me a "Sunday painter" and I was, when I had my job as a customs inspector. Sundays were the only days I had free to paint. Now, with the money I earn from teaching and selling my paintings, I don't need a full-time job anymore. Come with me. We'll explore Paris and I'll show you some of my favorite places, starting with the tollhouse where I used to work. Now you know why a poet friend of mine nicknamed me the Douanier, the customs inspector—a name that has stayed with me all these years! Come along now and if anyone should ask you who you're with, you can tell them: the painter, Henri Julien

ROUSSEAU

I was born in 1844 in the beautiful city of Laval. Where is that, you ask? On the road that leads from Paris to Brittany. We lived in the heart of the old town, at the foot of the castle. Even then, I wanted to become an artist. I would have liked to spend my time painting and playing the violin, but, because my parents were so poor, I had to begin work when I was very young. And when I was only seven years old, we lost the house because of my father's debts. My family moved away, and I stayed with relatives so that I could continue to attend the Laval School. I was not a very good student, except in drawing and music. Although these were difficult years for me, they taught me self-reliance. And so, when I realized I wanted to be a painter, I didn't try to find someone to teach me—I decided to learn by myself.

Turn back one page to see Rousseau's self-portrait. In this painting, entitled Myself: Portrait-Landscape, *Rousseau depicts himself as the traditional artist, somber and dignified, dressed all in black with a beret. He displays his palette and brush like a soldier presenting arms. The palette bears two names: that of Clémence, his first wife, who died in 1888; and Joséphine, whom he married in 1899. When the painting was exhibited for the first time, the public laughed and journalists made fun of it. One wrote: "He has painted himself the size of a midget, with an enormous head, filled, perhaps, with profound thoughts. . . ." Yet here Rousseau created a highly original view of both himself and his beloved Paris, with the world-famous Eiffel Tower in the background and a festive ship bedecked with colorful flags at its mooring on the Seine River.*

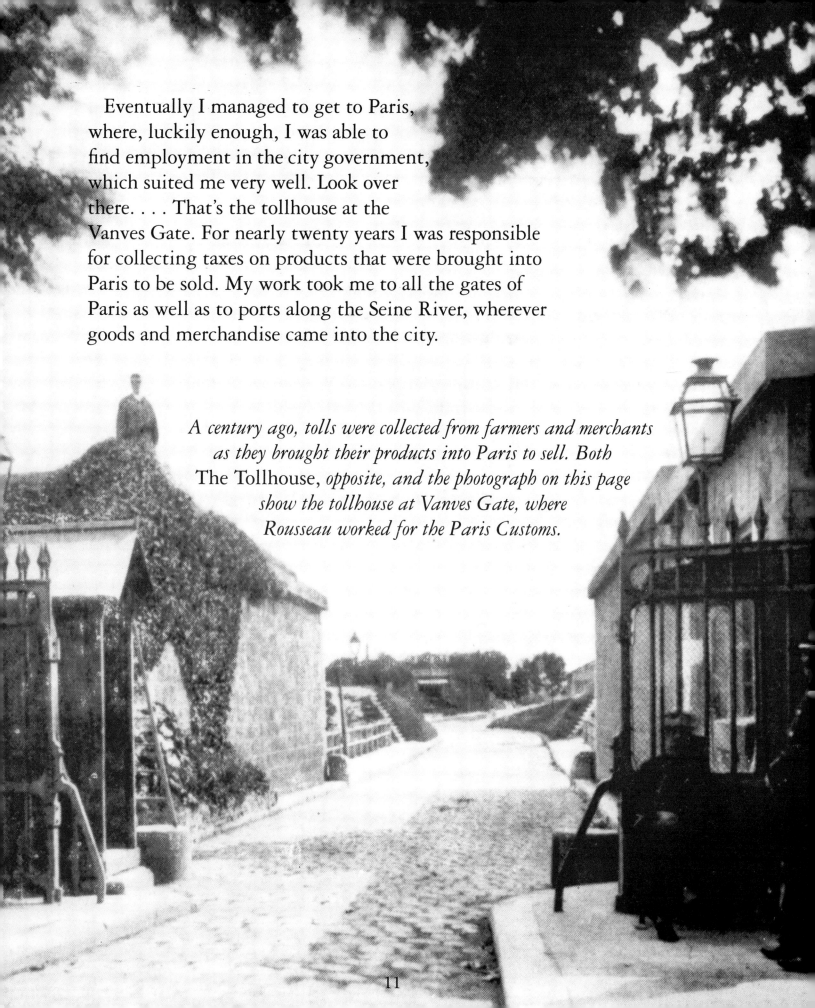

Eventually I managed to get to Paris, where, luckily enough, I was able to find employment in the city government, which suited me very well. Look over there. . . . That's the tollhouse at the Vanves Gate. For nearly twenty years I was responsible for collecting taxes on products that were brought into Paris to be sold. My work took me to all the gates of Paris as well as to ports along the Seine River, wherever goods and merchandise came into the city.

A century ago, tolls were collected from farmers and merchants as they brought their products into Paris to sell. Both The Tollhouse, *opposite, and the photograph on this page show the tollhouse at Vanves Gate, where Rousseau worked for the Paris Customs.*

This job left me with lots of spare time. Mostly very few carriages and boats came by, so my fellow workers would play cards or tell each other stories. As for me, I spent the hours observing the countryside and taking note of its contours, colors, and shapes. At home, on days when I wasn't working, I would make paintings of the things I had seen. I always began at the very top of the canvas and transferred the image from my mind to its surface, little by little, until I reached the bottom. Often it would take me several days, several Sundays. . . . This is how I taught myself to paint. When my superiors were kind enough to encourage my work and assign me to a tollhouse with a scenic view, I was even able to paint during my working hours. I painted what I saw in front of me: a sentry box and the fortifications that surrounded Paris; or the Seine, its banks, and its boats. I painted the Vanves Gate, Notre Dame Cathedral, the Île Saint-Louis, the Eiffel Tower, the Sèvres Bridge, and the Grenelle Bridge with its Statue of Liberty—a smaller version of the one overlooking New York harbor in America. Yes, I love and always will love Paris. Why? Because it's a big city, filled with people, shops, sounds, and colors. Because it's the capital of the Republic of France and I love the Republic.

BANKS OF THE SEINE: *A peaceful scene near Paris: a sentry box, a fisherman in his boat, a wisp of smoke that crosses the sky as if to go visit the other two smokestacks on the opposite bank. Here, as at the tollhouse, all is calm and peaceful. No fighting, smuggling, or fear, although Rousseau did maintain that he occasionally saw a ghost. His day-to-day work was so peaceful and monotonous that his imagination took flight, expressing itself here in subtle and somber colors. Others might have done crossword puzzles; Rousseau became a painter.*

O glorious painter of the
Republican soul
Your name is the flag of the
proud Independents

*1884, a splendid year! In the spring,
posters appeared all over Paris, announcing
the soon-to-open* Salon des Indépendants.
The Salon des Artistes Français *was an
exhibition of art works chosen by a jury and
presented by the French Academy since 1737.
The* Salon des Indépendants *was an
exhibition of artists who worked outside of
the French Academy, and it allowed
Rousseau to exhibit his canvases to a public
who appreciated his enormous talent. Later,*
he celebrated this occasion with his painting, Liberty Inviting the Artists to
Exhibit at the 22nd Salon des Artistes Indépendants. *Flags flutter in the breeze,
above the trees. Artists, men and women both, having stepped down from their carts
and carriages with their works under their arms, form a procession. They are heralded
by two huge banners with the colors of France and Paris and
by Liberty, an angel trumpeting a welcome. In the center of the
foreground, a lion holds a list of impressive artists, including*

*Rousseau and his friends, between his paws. Jules
Dalou's statue, on the facing page, is located on the
Place de la Nation in Paris. Like the painting above,
it celebrates the establishment of the French Republic—
a time of progress, justice, and abundance after long
years of upheaval and war.*

And why do I love the Republic, you ask? Because I love liberty, justice, peace, and the promise of a better world where brotherhood is the order of the day. I love Paris because it is the capital of the arts, the city where great artists live, and where, each year, they hold a great celebration of art called the *Salon des Artistes Français,* the official art exhibition, known as the Salon.

My fondest dream was to have my paintings exhibited there. Why, the president of the Republic himself opened that Salon! Everyone knew it was *the* great event for art and artists. Each year, the exhibition included paintings by the most famous painters, the ones with the elegant houses and impressive studios. I so much wanted to be part of it . . . but the powerful academics who made up the jury excluded me. They laughed at me because I did not go to the School of Fine Arts!

The Salon may well have been an important, government-sponsored event, but is was also a crowded, noisy affair, as you can see in this painting by Henri Gervex, who was one of the famous painters of the day. His painting is called A Meeting of the Jury of Painting at the Salon des Artistes Français *(1883).*

And so instead I showed my work at a different exhibition called the *Salon des Indépendants,* as I have done every year since it was created in 1884. This is how I became famous, you see. You musn't think that people don't know me. You might even say that I'm a celebrity because, each year, the critics discuss the works I exhibit. It is true that they often laugh and make fun of them. Still, they seek out my paintings, amidst the great many others exhibited there. My canvases are different. No one paints the way I do.

Picasso paid a few francs for this painting of Rousseau's. He was probably amused by its grandiose title: Representatives of Foreign Powers Come to Salute the Republic in a Gesture of Peace. *At last, a work of Rousseau's was received with acclaim, and the painter had to cope with crowds of admirers.*

A practical joker with a great fondness for Rousseau, Picasso is shown in the photograph below holding Rousseau's Self-Portrait with Oil-Lamp. *Here the artist has made himself look serious and dignified, like a scholar! The high forehead indicates great intelligence; the mustache and bushy eyebrows, a forceful and determined character. In reality, this portrait probably looked very little like Rousseau, who had a gentle air about him and always looked a little bit lost! In any case, it must have been one of Picasso's favorites because he kept it in his personal collection throughout his life.*

    *With rifles and sabers stacked like the poles of a tepee,
The Artillerymen look as though they're posing for a
group photograph. Count them: fourteen artillerymen, all
with the same face, like so many toy soldiers. These brave
soldiers are really fourteen Rousseaus—with minor
variations in equipment and stance—drawn from the
artist's imagination.*

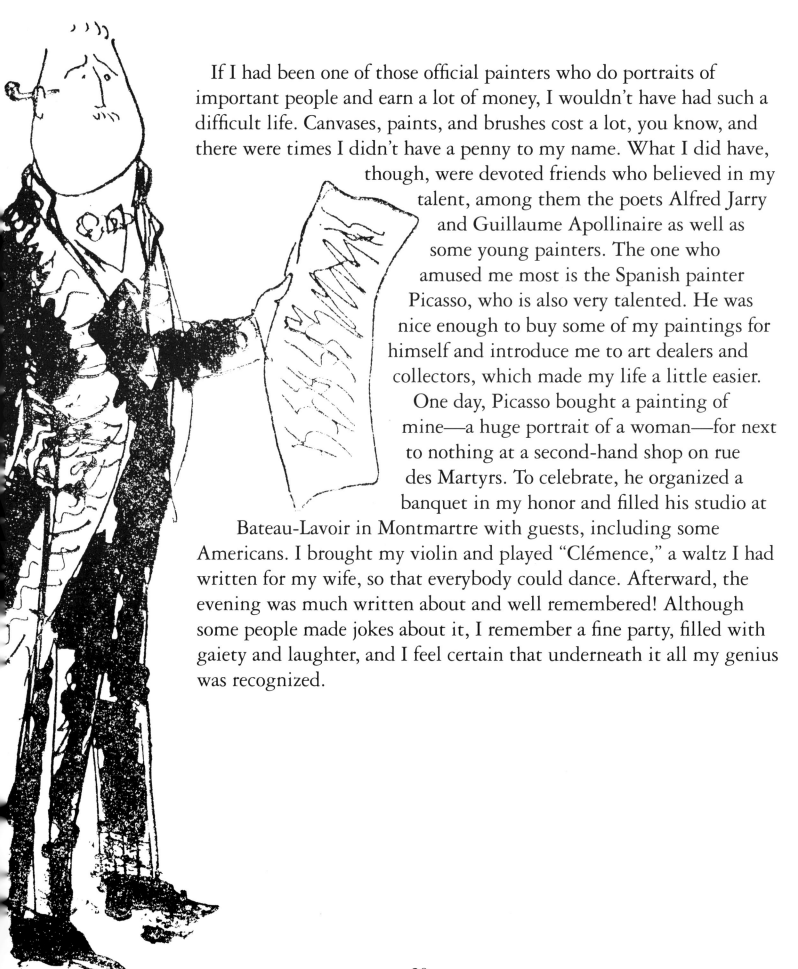

If I had been one of those official painters who do portraits of important people and earn a lot of money, I wouldn't have had such a difficult life. Canvases, paints, and brushes cost a lot, you know, and there were times I didn't have a penny to my name. What I did have, though, were devoted friends who believed in my talent, among them the poets Alfred Jarry and Guillaume Apollinaire as well as some young painters. The one who amused me most is the Spanish painter Picasso, who is also very talented. He was nice enough to buy some of my paintings for himself and introduce me to art dealers and collectors, which made my life a little easier.

One day, Picasso bought a painting of mine—a huge portrait of a woman—for next to nothing at a second-hand shop on rue des Martyrs. To celebrate, he organized a banquet in my honor and filled his studio at Bateau-Lavoir in Montmartre with guests, including some Americans. I brought my violin and played "Clémence," a waltz I had written for my wife, so that everybody could dance. Afterward, the evening was much written about and well remembered! Although some people made jokes about it, I remember a fine party, filled with gaiety and laughter, and I feel certain that underneath it all my genius was recognized.

Moved by the affection the poet Apollinaire had for him, Rousseau painted his portrait, The Muse Inspiring the Poet. *Apollinaire, dressed in his best suit, stands behind a row of sweet william with Marie Laurencin, a painter and the woman he loved. She points to the heavens, source of all inspiration. The sitting was not an easy affair. Apollinaire laughingly recalled that the painter took a tape measure and measured "my nose, my mouth, my ears, my forehead, my hands, my whole body," and entered the measurements in a notebook with all the concentration of a tailor. Once the portrait was finished, Rousseau had it framed and brought it to Apollinaire, who promptly flew into a rage. He thought it made him look ugly and his muse, uglier still.*

However, upon hearing all his friends tell him that the portrait bore him a strong resemblance, he changed his mind. These poets, painters, writers, and art dealers were all young and never missed an opportunity for fun, as you can see by looking at the caricature by Picasso on the opposite page, Apollinaire as an Academic— *a far cry from the actual character of Apollinaire! Picasso once bought a large painting by Rousseau for the small sum of five francs. Pleased with his purchase, the mischievous Spaniard planned a banquet in honor of the Douanier. Many people came—friends, hangers-on, and even some strangers—but the food itself never arrived! Alas, Picasso, in his excitement, had given the wrong date when ordering the meal! Finally, they used what they had and made a gigantic paella, a traditional Spanish rice dish, and all sat down to eat, drink, and sing.*

We're gathered together to honor Rousseau
Picasso pours wine—long may it flow!
And now let's stand, our glasses raised,
And sing to the world, "Rousseau be praised!"

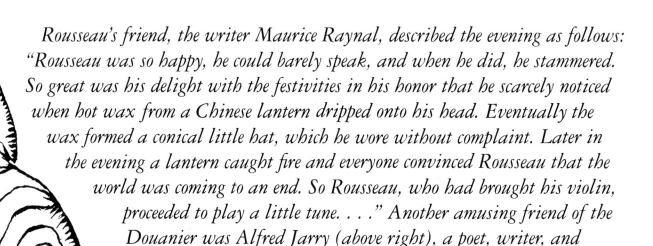

Rousseau's friend, the writer Maurice Raynal, described the evening as follows: "Rousseau was so happy, he could barely speak, and when he did, he stammered. So great was his delight with the festivities in his honor that he scarcely noticed when hot wax from a Chinese lantern dripped onto his head. Eventually the wax formed a conical little hat, which he wore without complaint. Later in the evening a lantern caught fire and everyone convinced Rousseau that the world was coming to an end. So Rousseau, who had brought his violin, proceeded to play a little tune. . . ." Another amusing friend of the Douanier was Alfred Jarry (above right), a poet, writer, and playwright. Much younger than Rousseau, with a sharp sense of humor that knew no bounds, he is perhaps best known for his play Ubu Roi, *for which he created the character Père Ubu, pictured at left. A play that caused a great sensation,* Ubu Roi *opened in 1896. Rousseau once made a portrait of his friend Jarry with an owl perched on his shoulder, which Jarry eventually destroyed . . . another unflattering portrait, perhaps?*

All my life—whether I was a student, a sergeant, or a customs inspector—people called me a dreamer, as if that were something bad. . . . But I've always felt that it's good to dream and to make up stories. When I make a painting, I am not trying to produce a photograph. I paint to create images that a camera would never see. When I paint a landscape, I reinvent the scene. When I paint a portrait, I'm not interested in rendering an exact likeness. Nonetheless, the person is always recognizable because I scatter my paintings with clues that help reveal his or her identity. Look, for instance, at this portrait of Pierre Loti, a novelist I like very much. A great world-traveler, he has been a member of the French Academy since 1891. Look at him closely: You can tell who he is because of the cat, the cigarette between his fingers (an unusual touch in a portrait and one that reveals his self-assuredness), and the fez he wears because some of his books are about the faraway lands of Islam.

The Football Players: *This is the title Rousseau gave to the painting on the opposite page, which shows the players in a luminous autumn landscape. But look closely—what shape is the ball? Do the players look as though they're playing with their feet or with their hands? It doesn't look like a football game, does it? It looks more like a rugby game. Rugby had just been introduced as a sport in France. Rousseau seems to have reinvented not only the game but the players as well. They could be dancers in a ballet or puppets on invisible strings, their movements frozen in time like the marionette held by the blond, chubby-cheeked child depicted above in* Child with Puppet. *Has the Douanier portrayed himself in these pictures? Is he the jumping jack with the big handlebar mustache? Or the child so lost in thought that he's forgotten to smile?*

24

Do you remember the *Portrait-Landscape* I showed you earlier? In that scene I planted myself like a tree in front of a Parisian landscape—that's why I gave the painting that name. In the background, you can see the Eiffel Tower. Imagine! I'm the first painter who ever put the Eiffel Tower in a painting! I see Paris changing from year to year, becoming more modern all the time. For me, that tower of steel—taller even than Notre Dame Cathedral—symbolizes the rising hope for a better life through progress. I believe that our intelligence will enable mankind to invent new technologies that will make life easier for all, and I'm sure that in doing so we will grow more wise, just, and kindly toward one another.

Rousseau believed that technical progress would bring everyone in the young French republic an opportunity for a better life. He was dazzled by the World's Fair of 1878 and even more so by the one of 1900, pictured in the photograph on these two pages. The riverbanks of the Seine were transformed by this exhibition, which gave everyone a glimpse of foreign lands as well as of the very first flying machines, like the one pictured above in Rousseau's The Fishermen and the Biplane.

This looks like a votive offering that a sailor might have painted in thanks for having weathered a terrifying storm at sea. In reality, Ship in a Storm is Rousseau's tribute to the glory of the French navy since it depicts the ultramodern warship, d'Entrecasteaux, which was launched in 1896.

He engraved on a bench near the Porte Dauphine
The two names he loved: Clémence and Joséphine

On Sundays, my wife and I liked to go to the Luxembourg Gardens, which are right nearby. I've always loved the country, even though I've lived in Paris for more than forty years without ever taking a vacation and only an occasional trip. My friend Apollinaire, who likes to make up stories, has everyone thinking that I've traveled a lot and that I went to Mexico. He even says that I met Emperor Maximilian of Austria there and saw that "Aztec landscape" with my own eyes. It is true that the fair-haired emperor was installed on the Mexican throne by Louis Napoleon and, incidentally, later shot to death by a firing squad. But as for the rest, it's pure fantasy, I assure you! Be patient and I'll tell you how I actually did come to know those faraway lands and their tropical forests. Now, I want to tell you about excursions closer to home.

My wife and I enjoyed visiting the countryside just outside of Paris.
I would bring my easel, brushes, and a box of paints and paint those
landscapes that caught my eye, much as did those painters who called
themselves "the impressionists" and first began to exhibit when I
was about twenty years old. It feels good to be out in the
countryside in front of an easel. Close your eyes and imagine:
There is a warm sun and a refreshing little breeze; a dog
approaches but doesn't dare get close enough to see what I'm
painting. There's a basket at my side, with a picnic in it—some
pâté, bread, and a bottle of wine. . . .

Those self-important academic painters whose works hung in the grand Salon painted enormous canvases, depicting battles with dozens of horses, scenes from Greek or Roman antiquity, stories taken from the Bible or the gospel. In just one painting they had to demonstrate all they knew: difficult compositions with deep perspective, a tangle of architecture, people in complicated poses. It was as if they had to pass an exam or win a contest. I think it's much more noble to paint what I paint: a fisherman like the one you see here in a detail from *The Chair Factory*, a wheel turning, or even the cat on the opposite page—a little scary, but peaceful at the same time. I'm sure you recognize him—he's the same one who sits next to Pierre Loti.

The Douanier Rousseau was known for his kindness and hospitality. He liked to entertain neighbors and friends in his studio. On these festive occasions, he would play his violin and sing songs he wrote himself. Look again at the previous pages, which reveal Rousseau's appreciation for the countryside. On page 28 is The Painter and his Model *and on page 29 is* The Cart of Père Juniet. *Monsieur Juniet was Rousseau's greengrocer, who also enjoyed Sunday outings with his family, riding in a cart drawn by a beautiful dappled mare named Rosa.*

Rousseau often filled his paintings with vegetation—sometimes familiar, like that shown here in The Walk in the Forest, and sometimes tropical and exotic, as in The Hungry Lion on the opposite page. The forest fascinated Rousseau and inspired him to transform nature into strange and even disquieting scenes.

When I paint a scene with wild animals and exotic plants, I imagine faraway countries where I have never been and that I only know from the botanical gardens and the zoo right here in the city of Paris. You know by now that I'm not much of a traveler, so why are my jungle scenes so convincing, you ask? Because I remember stories I've been told, photographs I've seen, and paintings by other artists who *have* traveled. You cannot imagine the powerful effect it had on me to see the collection of exotic images in a book called *Around the World.* Each page transported me far away and frightened me at the same time. These detailed illustrations showed nature all around the world—from the largest, most ferocious beast to the smallest and most delicate of plants. At the World's Fairs held here in Paris, I've also had the good fortune to observe people, plants, and animals from South America, Africa, and Asia. These were my most wonderful journeys.

Maybe what my paintings show is this: You don't have to *be* far away to *see* far away. I travel by using my imagination and my paintings, and if people don't understand that, it's too bad for them!

When I called this painting *Surprise!*, I hardly thought that the title might also apply to the critics and viewers who saw it at the *Salon des Indépendants,* where it was exhibited in 1891. It wasn't that this was the first time they had ever seen a wild beast in a painting; for some time, adventuresome artists had been traveling great distances to paint exotic landscapes and bring them back for people who only dream of traveling. It was that no one had ever seen a painting quite like this one: In a virgin forest dense with vegetation, a tiger is frozen mid-crouch. He seems to hesitate, uncertain whether to flee or to leap on whatever has taken him by surprise. Perhaps he has been napping, his belly full after a large meal. . . .

The Douanier often said that he experienced fear when he went to the Paris zoo to see the wild animals there. Many of his paintings reflect that emotion. For instance, in Surprise! on the opposite page, it is easy to imagine all kinds of frightening things happening in that dense, stormy jungle, where even the trees, with their blade-like leaves, are menacing. You might ask yourself, who is surprised? The tiger, an unseen explorer, or the painter himself? The exotic landscape of The Repast of the Lion, above, is much more peaceful, with its fantastical flowers and verdant trees and grasses bathed in warm moonlight. Here there is only the lion to fear.

The engraving on the opposite page, taken from *Around the World* shows tropical vegetation somewhere in Indochina. On top of it, I have superimposed my painting *The Snake Charmer*, so that you can see precisely the source of my inspiration. Later on, for other paintings, I turned to an animal book for children published by the Galeries Lafayette department store. Called *Wild Animals,* it has two hundred photographs of animals and descriptions of the way they live. I've painted many exotic landscapes with lions, tigers, leopards, antelopes, and monkeys in them. Why do I like to paint wild animals, you ask? Let me think a moment. . . . Probably because I love nature and freedom. I dream of a world in which men and women will no longer be poor, living uncomfortably in the city, and forced to take tedious jobs just to make a living.

You recall, Rousseau, the Aztec landscape,
The forest where the mango and pineapple grew,
Monkeys spilled the juice of watermelons,
And the blond emperor they shot there.
The pictures that you paint, you saw in Mexico.

The Snake Charmer *on page 36 is without a doubt one of Rousseau's most famous paintings. Turn back to see the colorful detail of dense vegetation that flourishes near the snake charmer. Compare that to the engraving in the background: Can you see that the foliage pictured here is equally as impenetrable? "When I step into those hothouses filled with strange plants from faraway lands, I feel as though I'm stepping into a dream," Rousseau said of the Paris Botanical Gardens. It's clear that this extraordinary vegetation— which is the main focus of the painting—was inspired by his regular visits to the hothouses there. The pink flamingo, above, another detail from the same painting, shows that dreams reinvent animals as well as plants. And what do you think of the owl on the facing page, staring out at you from his perch in the foliage in this detail from* The Hungry Lion?

Since I've become an old man, I've realized that life is a journey and that, like all journeys, mine will come to an end one day. I've had struggles along the way, to be sure, including financial difficulties and lack of recognition of my artistic efforts. I learned everything on my own and was able to paint what I wanted because I ignored those who laughed at me, and I persevered. It's now 1910, and modern young painters and poets sing my praises and consider me to be one of them. I have no doubt that my daughter, Julia, will be proud of me—one day my paintings will hang in important museums around the world, and the recognition and glory that have eluded me will be mine at last.

Animals in the jungle kill by necessity. It's a question of survival: The strong survive by devouring the weak who in turn devour those weaker than themselves. But why do men kill one another? Rousseau's nightmare vision of what happens when they do is shown in his painting War *on the following pages.* War, *an unstoppable force in a ragged white dress, rides an immense black horse at full gallop across a dead landscape littered with bodies. This picture conveys the devastation that war inevitably brings—even nature has been destroyed.*

Come with me now to the studio and I'll show you my latest exotic painting, which I plan to take to the *Salon des Indépendants* tomorrow. It's called *The Dream*. That simple, magical word is the best advice I can give you. You may be surprised to see a woman on a couch in the middle of a forest. But this is a dream, you see, and she is the one dreaming. The woman fell asleep on the couch at home, and now she dreams that she has been transported to an enchanted garden. Listen to the poem I wrote about it:

Yadwigha, peacefully asleep,
Enjoys a beautiful dream:
A snake charmer's pipe
Leaves music in the air,
While flowers and trees
Glisten in the moonlight.
Wild serpents, spellbound,
Are enchanted by the tune.

I know that this does not look like a real forest at all. I could have used photographs and engravings to make my forest realistic, had I wished to do so, but this is my vision of Eden. I have painted a contented woman, happily dreaming of paradise.

Before you go, let me show you one last dream. This one is called *The Sleeping Gypsy*. A wandering mandolin-player, exhausted by her travels, has fallen into a deep sleep. A lion gently sniffs at her, but does her no harm. She is safe as she sleeps in a world of my creation.

It makes me happy to have painted the images in my dreams and to have been able to show them to you. I hope that you will dream, too, as you look at my paintings. And when you are sad, as everyone is sometimes, you will only have to close your eyes to create a magical world where you are the ruler. In my paintings, I am the master of an enchanted universe where I will wait for you.

WHERE TO SEE ROUSSEAU

Rousseau would be pleased to know that today his works hang in museums around the world. You can go see his paintings as well as those of some of his friends, Pablo Picasso and Robert and Sonia Delaunay in the following places:

UNITED STATES
District of Columbia

Surrounded by gardens on the mall near Washington's capitol building, stands the National Gallery of Art. Here you can get to know *Boy on the Rocks*, an unusual portrait of a small, serious boy dressed in black and white, as well as several of Rousseau's well-known forest paintings *Tropical Forest with Monkeys*, reproduced on the cover of this book, *Equatorial Jungle,* and *Rendezvous in the Forest.* Not far away, in the Phillips Collection, you can see a lovely view of Paris called *Notre Dame: View of the Île Saint Louis from the Quay Henri IV.*

California

The Norton Simon Art Foundation in Pasadena has a well-known jungle painting with monkeys, entitled *Exotic Landscape*. At the Los Angeles County Museum of Art you will find *The French Republic,* which Rousseau painted in 1904.

Illinois

On Michigan Avenue, near Chicago's lakefront, is the Art Institute of Chicago, its entrance flanked by two lordly lions—a touch Rousseau would surely have appreciated and enjoyed. Here you can admire *The Sawmill, Outskirts of Paris, The Waterfall,* and *Dahlias and Daisies in a Vase.*

New York

New York City's museums have quite a few of Rousseau's most exciting paintings. One of your first stops should be the Solomon Guggenheim Museum, a cream-colored, hive-shaped building designed by Frank Lloyd Wright, which spirals up from the avenue to overlook Central Park. Here you can see *The Artillerymen* (page 19) and *The Football Players* (page 25). If you walk south along Fifth Avenue until you reach Eighty-second Street, you will come to the huge Metropolitan Museum of Art where you can see *The Repast of the Lion* (page 35) and *Banks of the Bièvre near Bicêtre, Spring.*

Just off Fifth Avenue in midtown Manhattan is the world-famous Museum of Modern Art with its vast and exuberant collection. You may want to sit for awhile in the museum's lovely sculpture garden before seeking out *The Dream* (pages 46-47) and *The Sleeping Gypsy* (page 49).

Outside of New York City, the Albright-Knox Art Gallery in Buffalo has a still life called *Flowers in a Vase.*

Massachusetts

If you're in the Boston area, you will want to spend a day at the Museum of Fine Arts. They have the painting *Lake of Geneva (Lac Léman).* You should also stop in at the Fogg Art Museum on the Harvard University Campus in Cambridge, where you will find *The Banks of the Oise River*, which Rousseau painted in 1907.

Michigan

The Detroit Institute of the Arts has two works by Rousseau, *Vase of Flowers* and *The Outskirts of Paris.*

Ohio

At the Cleveland Museum of Art, you can see the exciting painting *The Jungle: Tiger Attacking a Buffalo.*

Pennsylvania

If you get the chance to visit Philadelphia, stop in at the Philadelphia Museum of Art and see its wonderful collection. They have two paintings by Rousseau: *A Carnival Evening* and the amusing *Merry Jesters*.

The Museum of Art, Carnegie Institute, in Pittsburgh has the painting *House on the Outskirts of Paris,* and at the Barnes Foundation in Merion you will find *Unwelcome Surprise*, *The Present and the Past,* and *Woman Walking in an Exotic Forest.*

Virginia

The Virginia Museum of Fine Arts in Richmond has the scene *Tropical Landscape: An American Indian Struggling with an Ape.*

FRANCE
Paris

If you are lucky enough to go to Paris one day, you have only to take a walk across the bridges of the Seine and look down on the riverbanks to see the city that Rousseau loved.

You should visit the exciting Musée d'Orsay. This museum, devoted to nineteenth-century art, is one of the most important in Paris. Originally a railroad station, the building was erected in the center of Paris, on the left bank of the Seine, for the World's Fair of 1900. The museum houses two of the artist's most famous paintings: *War,* reproduced on pages 44–45, and *The Snake Charmer* (page 36).

At the Musée de l'Orangerie in the beautiful Tuileries Gardens, you will find nine of the Douanier's paintings, including *The Fishermen and The Biplane* and *Ship in a Storm* (both on page 27), *The Cart of Père Juniet* (page 29), and *The Chair Factory,* shown in the detail on page 30.

Your trip wouldn't be complete without a visit to the famous Musée du Louvre. You will remember that Picasso bought some of Rousseau's paintings. Two of these are now hanging in the Louvre. They are *Representatives of Foreign Powers Come to Salute the Republic as a Peaceful Gesture* (page 17), and *Self-Portrait with Oil-Lamp* (page 18).

ENGLAND
London

Some of Rousseau's works have even made their way across the English channel to London. You will find *Surprise!* at the National Gallery; the painting of *The Tollhouse (L'Octroi, page 34)* where Rousseau worked, at the Courtauld Institute Galleries; and *Bouquet of Flowers* at the Tate Gallery.

Happy hunting, and beware of the tigers!

IMPORTANT DATES
IN THE LIFE OF ROUSSEAU

1844   Birth in Laval, France, of Henri Julien Rousseau. His father is a poor tinsmith and Rousseau is forced to begin work at an early age. He is a mediocre student, excelling only in painting and music.

1852   His father's properties are seized, owing to financial difficulties and the family is forced to move away. The young Rousseau stays with relatives in Laval and attends the Laval School.

1864   Rousseau enlists in the 52nd Infantry.

1868   Rousseau's father dies. Rousseau obtains a discharge from the army in order to support his widowed mother.

1869   Rousseau marries his first wife, Clémence Boitard, the daughter of a furniture salesman, who will bear him nine children, all but two of whom die in infancy. Despite these tragedies, Rousseau referred to the twenty years he spent with Clémence as "the happiest of my life."

1871   Rousseau obtains a post as customs inspector. He is responsible for checking the contents of carriages entering the city. Wine, grain, milk, salt, and lamp oil are subject to taxes. It is a position with intermittent activity, leaving him time to pursue his interest in painting. He holds this position for twenty years.

1884   Opening of the *Salon des Artistes Indépendants*.

1886   Rousseau wheels four of his paintings through the streets of Paris in a handcart to exhibit them at the *Salon des Indépendants.* He will exhibit there nearly every year until his death.

1893   Rousseau retires from his post as customs inspector with an annual pension. He supplements his income with violin, painting, and singing lessons, composes a waltz and two plays, and organizes many small parties for his friends and neighbors. He meets Alfred Jarry, who is only twenty years old at the time and who, coincidentally, was also born in Laval. Jarry will become world famous as the author of the play "Ubu Roi," and is instrumental in launching Rousseau's career as an artist.

1900   Rousseau is dazzled by the Paris World's Fair. Impressed with modern technology, he believes in a brighter future for France.

1906   Jarry introduces Rousseau to the great poet Guillaume Apollinaire, who, in the beginning, is not impressed with Rousseau's paintings. Later on, he becomes one of Rousseau's greatest admirers and is inspired to write lyrical poems in his honor.

1908   An even more important introduction is made: Jarry arranges for Rousseau to meet Pablo Picasso, who takes to Rousseau and his work immediately. The banquet he gives later this year in honor of the Douanier is one of the highlights of Rousseau's life. Little by little a circle of great artists, including the painters Robert and Sonia Delaunay, and Fernand Léger, grows around him.

1910   Rousseau dies at the age of 64, having finally achieved the respect he sought as an artist. World wide recognition, however, does not come until some years after his death.

Apollinaire's epitaph for the tomb of the painter, Henri Rousseau, the Douanier

We salute you
Gentle Rousseau you can hear us
Delaunay his wife Monsieur Quéval and myself
Let our luggage pass duty free through the gates
    of heaven
We will bring you brushes paints and canvas
That you may spend your sacred leisure in the
    light of truth
Painting as you once did my portrait
Facing the stars

LIST OF ILLUSTRATIONS

In the following list, the titles and locations are given for works of art reproduced in this book.
A work's dimensions are given in both inches and centimeters, first by height, then width.
The quotations on pages 5, 14, 22, 28, and 40 are excerpts from poems by Guillaume Apollinaire.
Note: the abbreviation RMN stands for Réunion des Musées Nationaux.

Cover:
Tropical Forest with Monkeys, 1910. Oil on canvas, 51 x 64 in. (130 x 163 cm.). National Gallery of
Art, Washington, D.C. John Hay Whitney Collection.

Title Page
Detail of *The Snake Charmer,* page 36.

pages 4–5
The Kite, 1910. Photograph by Jacques-Henri Lartigue, courtesy of the Photo Association of the
friends of J.-H. Lartigue, Paris, France.

page 6
Myself: Portrait-Landscape, 1890. Oil on canvas, 56⁵⁄₁₆ x 43⁵⁄₁₆ in. (143 x 110 cm.). National Gallery of
Prague, Czechoslovakia. Photo courtesy of André Held, Ecublens.

page 8
Detail of *Liberty Inviting the Artists to Exhibit at the 22nd Salon des Artistes Indépendants,* page 14.

page 9
Detail of *Myself: Portrait-Landscape,* page 6.

page 10
The Tollhouse, 1890. Oil on canvas, 14¾ x 12½ in. (37.5 x 32 cm.). Courtauld Institute, London,
England. Photo courtesy of Giraudon.

pages 10–11
The Tollhouse at Vanves Gate, photograph by Eugène Atget, courtesy of Skira Archives.

page 12
Illustration for official and commercial publications, from the Deberny and Peignot Foundry, 1890.

page 13

Banks of the Seine, 1898. Oil on canvas, 12¾ x 15¾ in. (32.5 x 40 cm.). Muse d'Arte, Lugano, Switzerland.

page 14

Liberty Inviting the Artists to Exhibit at the 22nd Salon des Artistes Indépendants, 1906. Oil on Canvas, 68⅞ x 46½ in. (175 x 118 cm.). Museum of Modern Art, Tokyo, Japan. Photo courtesy of Skira Archives.

page 15

Aimé-Jules Dalou, (1838–1902). *The Triumph of the Republic,* 1879–1899. Bronze, 41¼ x 21¼ x 38¼ in. (12.6 x 6.5 x 12 cm.). Place de la Nation, Paris, France. Photo courtesy of Hirmer Verlag, Munich.

page 16

Henri Gervex, (1852–1929). *A Meeting of the Jury of Painting at the Salon des Artistes Français.* Musée d'Orsay, Paris, France. Photo courtesy of RMN.

page 17

Representatives of Foreign Powers Come to Salute the Republic in a Gesture of Peace, 1907. Oil on canvas, 51¼ x 63⅜ in. (130 x 161 cm.). Musée du Louvre, Paris, France. Pablo Picasso Collection. Photo courtesy of RMN.

page 18

Self-Portrait with Oil-Lamp, circa 1900–1903. Oil on canvas, 9½ x 7½ in. (24 x 19 cm.). Musée du Louvre, Paris, France. Pablo Picasso Collection. Photo courtesy of RMN.

Picasso holding two portraits by Douanier Rousseau. Photograph by André Gomès.

page 19

The Artillerymen, circa 1893–94. Oil on canvas, 31⅛ x 39 in. (72 x 90 cm.). The Solomon R. Guggenheim Museum, New York, New York.

page 20

Pablo Picasso (1881–1973). *Apollinaire as an Academic*, detail, 1910. Ink drawing. Photo courtesy of Skira Archives.

page 21

The Muse Inspiring the Poet, 1910. Oil on canvas, 57½ x 38⅛ in. (156 x 97 cm.). Kunstmuseum, Basel, Switzerland. Photo courtesy of Giraudon.

page 22

Lucien Lantier. Portrait of Alfred Jarry at the time he wrote "Ubu Roi," 1896. Engraving.

Alfred Jarry (1873–1907). Portrait of Père Ubu. Wood engraving.

page 23

Portrait of Pierre Loti, circa 1891. Oil on canvas, 24 x 19⅝ in. (62 x 50 cm.). Kunsthaus, Zurich, Switzerland.

page 24

Child with Puppet, 1903. Oil on canvas, 39⅜ x 31⅞ in. (100 x 81 cm.). Kunstverein, Winterthur, Switzerland

Illustration for official and commercial publications from the foundry of Deberny and Peignot, 1890.

page 25

The Football Players, 1908. Oil on canvas, 39⅜ x 39 in. (100 x 91 cm.). The Solomon R. Guggenheim Museum, New York, New York.

pages 26–27

View of the Seine and Eiffel Tower during the Paris World's Fair of 1900. Photograph courtesy of Roger-Viollet.

page 27

The Fishermen and The Biplane, 1908. Oil on canvas, 18⅛ x 1½ in. (4 x 55 cm.). Musée de l'Orangerie, Paris, France. Photo courtesy of Giraudon.

Ship in a Storm, circa 1898. Oil on canvas, 21¼ x 25½ in. (54 x 65 cm.). Musée de l'Orangerie, Paris, France. Photo courtesy of RMN.

page 28

The Painter and his Model, circa 1900–1905. Oil on canvas, 18³⁄₁₆ x 22 in. (46.5 x 56 cm.). Centre Georges Pompidou, Musée national d'Art moderne, Paris, France. Photo courtesy of Skira Archives.

page 29

The Cart of Père Juniet, 1908. Oil on canvas, 38¼ x 50¾ in. (97 x 129 cm.). Musée de l'Orangerie, Paris, France. Photo courtesy of RMN.

Illustration for official and commercial publications, from the foundry of Deberny and Peignot, 1908.

page 30

The Chair Factory, detail, circa 1897. Oil on canvas, Musée de l'Orangerie, Paris, France. Photo courtesy of RMN.

page 31

Detail of *Portrait of Pierre Loti*, page 23.

page 32

The Walk in the Forest, circa 1886–1890. Oil on canvas, 27½ x 23⅜ in. (70 x 60 cm.). Kunsthaus, Zurich, Switzerland. Photo courtesy of Giraudon.

page 33

The Hungry Lion, 1905. Oil on canvas, 78¾ x 120 in. (200 x 300 cm.). Kunstmuseum, Basel, Switzerland. Photo courtesy of H. Hinz, Basel.

page 34

Surprise!, 1891. Oil on canvas, 50½ x 63½ in. (130 x 162 cm.). National Gallery, London, England.

page 35

The Repast of the Lion, circa 1905. Oil on canvas, 44⅜ x 63 in. (113.5 x 160 cm.). The Metropolitan Museum of Art, New York, New York. Photo courtesy of André Held, Ecublens.

page 36

The Snake Charmer, 1907. Oil on canvas, 68⅛ x 74¾ in. (169 x 189 cm.). Musée d'Orsay, Paris, France. Photo courtesy of RMN.

"Vegetation of Indochina." Engraving from *Tour du Monde—Nouveau Journal des Voyages,* 1885. Librairie Hachette, Paris, France. Photo courtesy of Skira Archives.

page 37

"A horned 'sajou' with mustache." Engraving from *Musée des Familles, Lectures du soir,* 1839. Photo courtesy of Skira Archives.

pages 38 and 40

Details of *The Snake Charmer,* page 36.

pages 38–39

"Interior of a hothouse," 1838. Engraving from *l'Album du Jardin des Plantes,* plate 18, Paris, France. Photo courtesy of Skira Archives.

page 41
Detail of *The Hungry Lion*, page 33.

page 42
Detail of *The Dream,* pages 46–47.

page 43
Detail of *War*, pages 44–45.

pages 44–45
War, 1894. Oil on canvas, 44⅛ x 76¾ in. (114 x 195 cm.). Musée d'Orsay, Paris, France. Photo courtesy of RMN.

pages 46–47
The Dream, 1910. Oil on canvas, 79½ x 117¾ in. (204.5 x 299 cm.). Museum of Modern Art, New York, New York.

page 49
The Sleeping Gypsy, 1897. Oil on canvas, 51 x 79 in. (129.5 x 200.5 cm.). Museum of Modern Art, New York, New York.

page 50
Illustration for official and commercial publications, from the foundry of Deberny and Peignot, 1860.

page 53
View of the Île Saint-Louis from Quai Henri IV, 1909. Oil on canvas, 13 x 16⅛ in. (33 x 41 cm.). The Phillips Collection, Washington, D.C.

page 54
The Douanier Rousseau. Photograph by Dornac, courtesy of the Larousse-Giraudon Archives.

page 57
The painter Rousseau in his studio. Photograph courtesy of Roger-Viollet.

pages 63 and 64
Illustrations for official and commercial publications, from the foundry of Deberny and Peignot, 1890.

First published in the United States of America in 1993 by
Rizzoli International Publications, Inc.
300 Park Avenue South
New York, New York 10010

Translated by Joan Knight

Library of Congress Cataloging-in-Publication Data

Plazy, Gilles, 1942–
    [Dimanche avec le Douanier Rousseau. English]
    A weekend with Rousseau / by Gilles Plazy.
        p.   cm.
    Summary: The nineteenth-century French painter who captured the
sights of Paris talks about his life and work as if entertaining the reader
for the weekend. Includes reproductions of the artist's work
and a list of museums where they are on display.
    ISBN 0-8478-1717-2
    1. Rousseau, Henri Julien Félix, 1844–1910—Juvenile literature.
2. Painters—France—Biography—Juvenile literature.   [1. Rousseau,
Henri Julien Félix, 1844–1910.   2. Artists.]   I. Title.   II. Title:
Weekend with Rousseau.
    ND553.R67A2   1993
    759.4—dc20   93–12187
                                                                      CIP
                                                                       AC

Design by Mary McBride

Printed in Italy